TOOLS FOR TEACHERS

- **ATOS:** 0.7
- **GRL:** C
- **WORD COUNT:** 39

- **CURRICULUM CONNECTIONS:** weather

Skills to Teach

- **HIGH-FREQUENCY WORDS:** have, in, is, it, the, they, we, will, your
- **CONTENT WORDS:** animals, boots, coats, clouds, cloudy, drink, drops, fall, grab, plants, play, rain, raindrops, umbrella, water(s), wear
- **PUNCTUATION:** exclamation points, periods, question mark
- **WORD STUDY:** long /e/, spelled y (cloudy, rainy); /oo/, spelled oo (good, boots); /ow/, spelled ou (clouds); compound word (raindrops); multisyllable words (animals, umbrella)
- **TEXT TYPE:** explanation

Before Reading Activities

- Read the title and give a simple statement of the main idea.
- Have students "walk" though the book and talk about what they see in the pictures.
- Introduce new vocabulary by having students predict the first letter and locate the word in the text.
- Discuss any unfamiliar concepts that are in the text.

After Reading Activities

The book's text mentions that plants need rain. Plants need water to grow. Plant seedlings in the classroom. Have the readers take turns watering them. Set the plants near a window. Explain that plants also need sunlight to grow. Have them record how they grow each day. What do they notice?

Tadpole Books are published by Jump!, 5357 Penn Avenue South, Minneapolis, MN 55419, www.jumplibrary.com

Copyright ©2019 Jump. International copyright reserved in all countries. No part of this book may be reproduced in any form without written permission from the publisher.

Editor: Jenna Trnka **Designer:** Anna Peterson

Photo Credits: Westend61/SuperStock, cover; Taeya18/Shutterstock, 1; marekuliasz/Shutterstock, 2–3, 16tm; andreiuc88/Shutterstock, 4–5; stanley45/iStock, 6–7, 16bl, 16bm; Wolfgang Kruck/Shutterstock, 8–9; Varina C/Shutterstock, 10, 11, 16tl, 16tr; emholk/iStock, 12–13; Tsomka/Shutterstock, 14–15, 16br.

Library of Congress Cataloging-in-Publication Data
Names: Kenan, Tessa, author.
Title: Rainy / by Tessa Kenan.
Description: Tadpole edition. | Minneapolis, MN : Jump!, Inc., (2018) | Series: Weather report | Includes index.
Identifiers: LCCN 2018006014 (print) | LCCN 2017061690 (ebook) | ISBN 9781641280112 (ebook) | ISBN 9781641280099 (hardcover : alk. paper) | ISBN 9781641280105 (pbk.)
Subjects: LCSH: Rain and rainfall—Juvenile literature. | Precipitation (Meteorology)—Juvenile literature.
Classification: LCC QC924.7 (print) | LCC QC924.7 .K46 2018 (ebook) | DDC 551.57/7—dc23
LC record available at https://lccn.loc.gov/2018006014

WEATHER REPORT

RAINY

by Tessa Kenan

TABLE OF CONTENTS

tadpole
books

RAINY

It is cloudy.

2

Will it rain?

Clouds have water drops.

They fall.

Rain is good.

It waters plants.

Animals drink it.

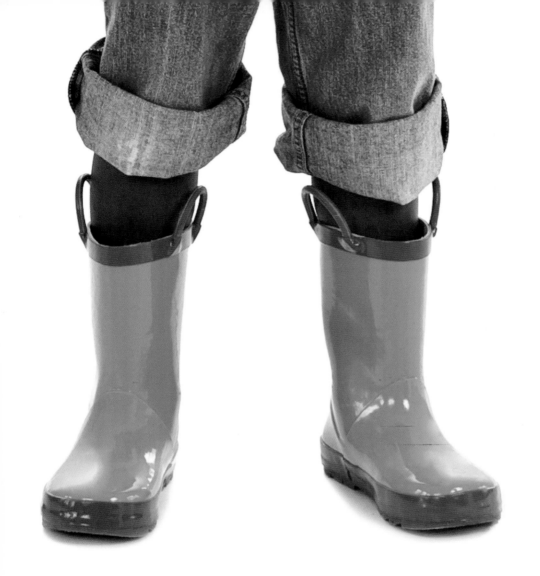

We wear boots.

We wear coats.

We play in the rain!

Grab your umbrella.

Feel the raindrops!

WORDS TO KNOW

boots

cloudy

coats

plants

raindrops

umbrella

INDEX

16